FLIES

or, the Last Days, D___h, and Putrefaction of Mr. Sam Jeden
as Narrated by Eight Generations of *Musca Domestica*

John Surowiecki

FLIES

FIRST EDITION, 2012

PRINTED IN THE USA

ISBN: 978-1-937027-01-8

DISTRIBUTED BY SMALL PRESS DISTRIBUTION

1341 SEVENTH ST.

BERKELEY, CA 94710

WWW.SPDBOOKS.ORG

THIS BOOK IS FUNDED IN PART BY A GRANT

FROM THE NATIONAL ENDOWMENT FOR THE ARTS.

UGLY DUCKLING PRESSE

THE OLD AMERICAN CAN FACTORY

232 THIRD ST., #E303

BROOKLYN, NY 11215

For Denise, who puts up with me.

Special thanks to Karen (Surowiecki) Grady for her undying Latin. And to Kate Young, Stefano Campiglio, Brian and Lisa Fitch, Joe Cary, Alyssa Mazzarella, and members of the Storrs Writers Group (Denise Abercrombie, Jon Andersen, Lisa Butler, Carol Chaput, Jim Coleman, Anne Flammang, Joan Joffe Hall, Ann Z. Leventhal and David Morse).

FLIES

[A fly] put in spirit of Wine, was very quickly seemingly kill'd, and both its eyes and mouth began to look very red, but upon the taking of it out, and suffering it to lie three or four hours, and heating it with the Sun beams cast through a Burning-glass, it again reviv'd, seeming, as it were, to have been all the intermediate time, but dead drunk, and after certain hours to grow fresh again and sober.

—Robert Hooke, *Micrographia*

Bee! I'm expecting you!
Was saying Yesterday
To Somebody you know
That you were due -

The Frogs got Home last Week -
Are settled, and at work -
Birds, mostly back -
The Clover warm and thick -

You'll get my Letter by
The seventeenth; reply
Or better, be with me -
Yours, Fly.

—Emily Dickinson, *No. 1035*

Proem

There is one god & D___h is his/her/its name.
Proof? Look around you: D___h is always in the air
(smelling of cantaloupe gone bad) & flies are 1/2 in
love w/him/her/it. D___h (we can't speak his/her/its
name) turns the world into food: & believe

it or not there are plenty of micronanocreatures who
see flies as their Sunday supper. O D___h
doesn't need our prayers & paeans. This is
a courtesy really, an opportunity
for the old bow & scrape. . . . . & for you,

human reader, it's a minicourse in flythropology,
a tiny wedge in the pie chart of flystory,
a glimpse into our small world in which you, like it
or not, aren't movers & shakers, kings & queens————but dinner.
Then again, humility breeds wisdom. So read on.

Fly No. 1

1

I, his amanuensis, guardian angel, Virgil- & Horatio-
to-be, don't get it: he sits & sits & sits & sits & sits
& doesn't die————————————————Why?
Isn't he our K-2 of cheap white bread? our super-
sized sopressata? our stuffed Christmas goose? Imagine

our delight when we 1st saw him, big tube of lard-
speckled *jus*-oozing meat————————& yet:
under those long old ears, fat at the narrows,
a ragged pulse stubbornly throbs in stolen time.
How can something so large

come from so small a life?
something this weight from
so much wasted time?
something this sweet from
something so sorrowful?

2

Muscae sunt omnes divisae in partes tres:
ɪ: head; ɪɪ: thorax; ɪɪɪ: abdomen.
Not to mention our *occhio composto*
& a labium that ends in a sponge to sop up
the vomit we make of the world.

We liquify and lap up the crumbs
of my man's life. . . . .
saltines, sardines, pork 'n beans:
eventually my man himself (that's the plan anyway).
We are so many & have been so many

& will be so many WE ARE NEVER ALONE
(————————*Sumus ergo sum*————————).
Patience, we say. Patience & more patience.
We may not live longer than a lunar month,
but each instant of flystory festers in each of us.

3

My man's rooms have been bugged, rebugged
& rerebugged w/my progeny & palzz
as well as the occasional invader, eg: vertiginous
brown hornets (all stinger/no brains),
doddering ladybugs, malcontent roaches,

malodorous silverfish, honeyless bees,
a minatory millipede on the floss & zit-eyed Herr
Schwartzspinne who thinks of me as a postcoital morsel
for his *liebchen*————————a monster who will devour
the little Nazzi as soon as she's done w/me.

Dietary Note: We prefer (in no particular order) blood,
crap, grease, suet, molasses, honey, fruit. But best of all:
☠ ☠ ☠ ☠ ☠ MUSCALURE ☠ ☠ ☠ ☠ ☠
aka (Z)-9-tricosene: sex pheromone & fly bait so irresistible
we gladly————& sadly————follow it to our graves.

4

Ants————not flies————mate *aviotrasportato*.
We are poor groundlings, humping away
in the deep shadows of cellars
& closets or among the
earthworms & dung beetles,

ticks & slugs* * * * * * * * * * * * * *
* * * * * * * * * * * * * * * * * * * *
* * * * * * * * * * * * * * * * * * * *
seeking out a leaf canopy or mud motel
under a teetering stone or amid the oats

of a poorly managed pantry,
beating our wings faster than we should
in the July heat (we can spasm into paralysis):
O O O a skip, a flutter, a twitch:
black balls of fire → smudges of black ash.

5
Pensées

1. No fly has ever committed murder (or suicide).

2. Really, what can we possibly do? Lick you to death?

3. We are all of a piece & always unconnected.

4. What 1 fly learns, another fly knows.

5. What 1 fly experiences, another fly calls upon.

6. A fly never sees another fly as an enemy.

7. Because our lives are so short, flies don't experience
   old age: our last days are pretty much like our first,
   maybe a little less bouncy and a lot less earnest: but
   no arthritis, no psoriasis about the elbows knees & dick,

   no athlete's foot, no sciatica, no prostate the size
   of a meatloaf, no gingivitis, no bone loss, no shingles.

8. There is no lord of the flies.

9. Every fly is remembered; none go down in history.

10. What are there more of: flies or poets?

6

From the trinity site of my man's snoring comes
in ptolemaic rings————————————————:
(i) Mziz Stanko's heavy foot above us (for we
live in her lima-bean-green house),
(ii) the *vroom, vroom, vroom* of drug traffic,

(iii) the *slop, slop, slop* of harbor slime,
(iv) the *click, click, click* of horseshoe crabs &
(v) the laughing *weep, weep, weep* of gulls. Then it's:
(vi) Perezz yelling at his wife or it's
(vii) his snot-smeared boys marching

to the lemon-ice stand or
(viii) never-wrong Wright
grunting *Finlandia*like in the john or
(ix) Frau Schwartzspinne, recently widowed,
yanking d___hwebs out of her bunghole.

7
Poem Shaped Like Mizzouri

We'll never know if the flies outside my
  man's room are more than the sum of their
    desperate appeals, visitors from Mizzou &/
    or Mizzizzippi—prisoners in the land of
    spiders & birds & *api industriose* (see *Pinocchio*

    Chap. xxiv & Proverbs Plate vii: "the busy bee
    has no time for sorrow") + assassin bugs & venus
    fly traps & demon-faced bats & the blue holocaust
    of bug zappers. They beg us to help them, but what
    can we do? None of us knows how we got here &

    none wants to know how to leave. There's no end
    to them: ultimately done w/, done in, done for.
    So sweet, tho, how the windowglass magnifies,
    how the sun touches us & the touch gives us

                              pause.

8

D___h has arrived by the back door in a meter-
reader's homely green & gray——————-&
I think he/she/it has come for me. Even my man
can smell the melon. The moon has become a pie,
a wart has become a lump, a lump a stone,

a wariness a sadness, a stiffness a paralysis, a last
glance at things a sweet vision of edenic filth,
of cities sinking into lovely lakes of sewage.
As for my man, my fateless, foeless, feckless Sam,
lonelier than ever in a no-fly-zone-to-be,

he can only snore & snort & fart & burp & grunt,
his fat hand by the framed photo of his wife
————————good-bye,————————
————————good-bye,————————
————————good-bye.

Fly No. 2

1

My man, Sam Jeden, beloved of beloved Stef
(now deceased), half-brother of artless Art
(also deceased), father of childless Eva (not deceased but
graying white trash in the great state of Flyrida),
brings home fungus-furred beans from the A&P +

wormy corn, 30-day Wonder & dark-hearted onions.
He's a cow of a man who's now & then a raging bull
(note that we aren't equipped to see red: redness & rage
are unknown to us). His eyebags are the indigo of iodine (I)
dripped on Idahos.

His heart is a carp, orange, flipflopping.
His lungs are Electrolux bags bursting w/soot (C) &
sand (Si) & rust (Fe) & common dross.
His memories of Stef are fading & this he understands to be
————————& rightly so—————————the beginning of his end.

2

His kidneys sparkle w/salts. He shakes. He drools.
He pisses on his shoes. He thinks. He has erections.
He thinks he has erections. He thinks of salvaging his life.
He reasons. He flounces. He staggers.
He trips. He falls. He feels pain. He feels remorse.

He feels——returning at last to the elements——nothing.
He spends afternoons trying to remember the name
of Stef's perfume: attar of lilies of the valley,
bells ringing out smells behind the machine shop,
dark green soldiers *v.* the soft green of May.

He'd lift her hair & kiss the nape & scape of her neck,
inhaling the scent* * * * *girlish & clean & bittersweet,
something like the day when spring 1st refuses
to oblige the cold w/its surrender————————when
air vibrates w/the heat that is, @ heart, itself.

3
L.S.M.F.T.

In the torn pocket
of my man's terrycloth robe
where he once kept his false teeth
he now keeps his Luckies:
to us, a patch of pollution

& acrid weather;
to him, the giddiness
of a tickled throat,
the warmth that spreads up & down
his upsidedown lungtree.

His lips push out O_2-less Os
& clouds shaped like
⇨⇨⇨⇨Hungary⇦⇦⇦⇦
——he spits, tongue-tip against lip-
top: *tih tih tih tih tih tih tih tih tih tih.*

4
Le Poème de l'extase

My man remembers. We don't. For us time = slime,
a runny camembert sliding by & touching & penetrating
itself: peninsulas slipping into bays, islands getting isthmused———;
he remembers wetting nicely pressed slacks w/gobs of semen while
imagining lovely Mziz Z____ in her shorts breathing hard &

writing in WD-40. She feels forlorn, unfaithful to the core but
SHE IS AFFIRMATION, SHE IS ECSTASY
so enjoying the close attention he pays
to her parts, her biological flanges, hinges, tubes——
——————————————————: is it all internal cum-

bustion, her organs like maracas or a swell of cellos
or the tremors of faults & plates passing thru?
His lips zip up her leg like a cowcatcher.
Her eyes squeeze shut. Her toes curl.
Her Duzz-red hands close on his arms like vices.

5

What am I buzzing in his ear? Sage advice, ie:
stop living. My man is a *fait*
accompli. Nothing he does anymore will be of any
consequence to anyone except maybe Mziz Stanko
who needs the rent $————————————What

is it that he does when he has nothing to do?
Well, he sits & sits & &c.
He reads the mysteries
Mziz Lucasz (local lending library lady) leaves.
He watches the news, power gained & lost (&

he sleeps thru watching or, as he
thinks, watches as he sleeps). Sometimes
the quick-to-rile Perezz will say hello or Wright
(heading johnward) will wave across the hall,
but they don't visit & they don't care.

6

During *our* last days our buzzo is a bit more basso &
we bump into things & spin in fitful circles, but
we remain ourselves, the sole fly, the whole fly,
while Sam——Sam is NOT the Sam
of his nightstand photo, NOT the

✪✪✪boy bombardier✪✪✪
w/his blushing bride, Stef, the magnificent Stef————!
She was the coat hanger & he the coat,
soggy & smelling of the dismal damp.
She was the piston, carburetor, generator & battery

& he a puff of CO- & CO_2- & H_2S-laden exhaust.
She was the sturdy white picket fence &
he the puny cucumber under browning leaves.
She was the picture, picture frame & non-
reflective glass & he the blank wall.

7
Little Eva

He dreams of his little girl as
she parades in her new blue dress.
He's the trombone following
———*wah wah wah wah*———;
he's the *oom pah pah* & *twiddley twiddley dee.*

He's the waltzing bear
so careful not to make
her head spin, her padded rump
secure in the crook of his arm.
Her voice is in his ear singing

ABCDEFGHIJK*MMMOP.*
He throws her into the air,
a bean bag, a June bug;
he carries her on his head,
a bunch of blue bananas.

8

Sam's pop, elbow-high buffer & grinder,
was the Z-shaped scar along Sam's chin
& the emptiness in his heart;
his mom was mostly d__d most of the time.
The old house is gone & the other houses are

in tears, staining themselves w/rust:
boo hoo boo hoo from the
round windows——*wah wah wah*
from the rectangular.
Sam & Art grew up surrounded by

⇨ ⇨ ⇨ ⇨ Hungarians ⇦ ⇦ ⇦ ⇦
who made their own flypaper, dipping 8.5 x 11 sheets
into a molten amalgam of white & brown sugar,
maple syrup & molasses & then, when the sheets
were still sticky, dusting them w/arsenic (As) (☠).

9
TKU, Frau Schwartzspinne, for Killing Me

Herr S is long *kaput*, a mere snack for Frau S, *hässlich*
emblem of retiary cruelty & endless appetite,
life-sucking beast hiding in her cyclone-shaped hotel,
patient like us (& more efficient). It appears I—gulp!—
misjudged a death-rope for a cobweb. Flotsam

everywhere & mummies! I'm fucked. Big time.
* * * * * * * * * * * * * * * * * * *
* * * * * * * * * * * * * * * * * * *
How could I have been so foolish?
Even a hornet would have had a clue:

Love = appetite. Life = eat or be eaten. Now I'm a parcel,
plainly wrapped in hard spit, my innards sucked up,
my exoskeleton endo-ing, my brain a kind of jam:
Endgame. *Auf wiedersehen*. It seems I am her little *pfeffernüsse*
! !

Fly No. 3

1

Sumus ergo sum. I understood my man Sam to be a
gentle oozy cow waiting to d_e, a dairy queen
w/sex drive in N & down a qt in testosterone ($C_{19}H_{28}O_2$).
Instead I find a weapon-wielding maniac w/20/20 eyes
(after a lifetime of ophthalmological waxy buildup).

I hide in drapery folds & light fixtures, waiting, waiting
for the swatter's whistle. Ahh but he's tired of the hunt
& is cut into his sofa like a petroglyph. The phone rings, wrong #:
at least it's not his daughter SOSing for $ or announcing she's in love
w/someone she's met at a bar who can put an olive into a

martini glass w/o touching it* * * * * * * * * *.
Is our man the very man who wouldn't kill a fly?
No way————————! He's a killing machine (turret-necked &
swiveling) & (to him) all we are are the murmurous haunts
& unlovely black pearls of summer afternoons.

2

There is no fly by night————————————:
I remain in a darkness of my own making, raisin among
raisins on a Kellogg's box, safe so long as he doesn't deploy
the Ω BOMB, ie, press the ↑ button & release the mist-
begotten cloud. INSTEAD OF D_ING, HE'S BECOME D___H!

O my brain reels w/quiddities. A fly flies: can a man man?
Yes————————————: *The man manned the man-of-*
war in a manly manner. The darkness gives me an eyesache.
The swatter is no longer on the coffee table. Sam no longer
sleeps. I hear the bumblebee bus buzz by. I hear the TV

————————*Man manhandles manicurist in Manchester*————————
but nothing of *my* man. Is he tiptoeing thru the tulips?
Does he, like the chameleon, eat only air?
What storm is that born in the east?
The rest is sil

Fly No. 4

1

D__ly d__ly light, a medley of swattings (my
predecessors & palzz, alas, black patties scooped
up in paper napkins & tossed into the trash) & later. . .
a preemptive 1st-use substrategic deployment of the Ω BOMB
under the sink & along ceiling/wall joints. His Ortho®finger is

now callused & fatigued, the fumatorium is no more.
Res judicata. How calm Sam is,
reading whodunnits in his graying
robe & boxers (TKU Mziz Lucasz for the mysteries, you
w/yr white hair & red face like an eclipse of the sun, so delighted

to visit, so happy to be of help). On tap for tonite:
PBR, *penne à la oleo* & mini-Mounds from an All
Hallows' Eve long since past. He will scratch his balls
in the blue glow of the TV & the searing white light
of a justice too prompt & too severe & too inflexible.

2

The bodycount is @ 15. *Res ipsa loquitor*: enough to make
my man a mass murderer—even as he naps the nap of babes.
When he's just up, pink in the new light, his blind hand groping
for his Raisin Bran; or at 10, when he's jelly-kneed outdoors,
eyeing disillusioned women in nightgowns as they bend over for

their *Posts*; or at 2 when he's on a bench watching
humpback harbor waves & wondering if anyone notices the shoes
rotting off his feet; or at 5 when he's walking back to Mziz Stanko's,
saying hello to young moms, adding rosaries of praiseful phrases
about their puffy children w/*kremska* in their pants & gutta-

percha leaking from their mouths: AT NO TIME will he give
his bloodlust any thought. In summary then:
✝ ✝ ✝ ✝ ✝ ✝ ✝ ✝ ✝ ✝ ✝ ✝ ✝ ✝ ✝
15 fly deaths = 0 human regrets/15,000,000 fly deaths = the same.
So————I have to ask: what did we do?

3

The swatter is speckled
w/the blood & viscera
of my generation. Murder
exhausts us who haven't
the luxury of retribution.

Why invite new pogroms
of swatting & spraying?
There's no *contrapasso* for flies.
You won't find a flykiller
so cleverly placed

& cleverly punished
in so clever an inferno.
For us, revenge is
only served spoiled.
Patience, patience, pat

Fly No. 5

1
Muscae Volitantes

My man's seeing things,
floaters & flashers, flies flying
in his vitreous humor
————(no joke!)————:
a patina on his retina

that might be interpreted
as endgame's last move.
At least he won't d_e like a fly,
ie——————————, riced
in swatters & screen doors,

sucked into fans, steam-scorched
on spaghetti nite, spinning in telescoping circles,
on an organophosphate $\{[(CH_3)_2CHO]CH_3P(O)F\}$
high? When Sam goes,
no one will see his going.

2
Flyographia Literaria

O we know about yr Shakespeare: a moon = a lantern;
a tempest-tossed sea = a quilt of trash-bags sewn together
w/stagehands dressed in black under it leaping up &
falling again to their knees. We know about Mziz Macbeth
& old man Lear, like my man Sam, but mad as a moth.

It's not S we rebuke, but the poet who contends that *Flea*,
not *Fly*, is the emblem of love! We lap, we spongebathe, we tickle
w/palps, & yet we're disallowed because in *Flea*
2 bloods mingled are——even tho *Flea* is drawn to milady's ankles
☞ BECAUSE SHE HASN'T BATHED IN 6 OR 7 YRS!

& *Flea* is never far from a rat's back,
sipping cocktails of swill, injecting plague
into lovely gams & depleting
the population of Europe by nearly 60%.
Love = D___h, says *Flea*. Love then D___h, says *Fly*.

3
Omphaloskepsis

Life slips away, leaving my man a slouched buddha,
chin hard on chest. He sees himself walking
to school w/brother Art. The harbor winds keep the snow @ bay.
Only a few flakes reach them.
Then————————————:

he's staring @ the apple-sized cherries of Stef's
kitchen wallpaper. Then————————: he's w/Stef on her last day
as she confounds the world's medicos by not having
any lungs to speak of: just a map in black & pink
of where they used to be.

He holds her hand. He knows she's leaving him.
Then————————: he looks up, thinking he might find her soul
hovering above: but all he sees are the ceiling tiles
& the soundproofing holes in them:
black stars in a white sky.

4
(Ag) $

My man dreams he's on his feet again calculating
a *mean free path* to the Silver Dollar [*(Ag) $*], Orpheus regardant,
Lazzarus redux————————————————————,
cavorting, laughing, w/just enough $ for a draft of PBR
or if he's lucky Zzimmerman the *très gallant* liquor salesman

will introduce him to an exciting new vodka from Yemen.
Or perhaps a woman in her 50s w/pity in her Irish eyes will buy
him a pint in memory of her brutal barfly Da————————.
He'll watch the game on the enormous TV,
Sox *v.* Sawx, then the news (war

is bad war is good war is war).
He'll stagger home————past the dark dead factory
where machines that made other machines were made:
brave, dauntless, steadfast, on his way to Mziz Stanko
(& to us).

5
D___h Strikes Again

O I see: D___h has come for me, not Sam.
Something I sponged up? Some unheard of taphonomical
phenomenon————? O well. What does it matter?
D___h: I am the Darwin to yr FitzRoy.
Let the voyage begin.

My man Sam will follow soon enough. A visiting nurse
has already visited, Mziz Lucasz has left her last LREQueen,
Wright has moved his bowels, Perezz is hushed,
Mziz Stanko sits in the poverty-stricken dark.
Did you know the common fly

originated on the steppes of central Asia? & the underside
of the male fly is yellowish like pus? & when Orestes leaves,
he takes w/him a city's sins, its d___d & its flies?
Fled is that wondrous music.
Do I sleep or stay awake?

Fly No. 6

1

The book of my man's life = an A&P flyer
glanced at, folded up, tossed into the trash,
recalled in infelicitous fits & spurts: today-only bargains,
2-for-1 specials, double-coupon bonanzas.
✂--

He eats food better eaten by other mouths,
breathes air better breathed by other lungs——& yet
he goes on: still alive, still alive, still alive-O——————,
so unlike us: our finales fit our size & place
in the universe: we end small: but we never end alone.

The kicker is: Sam could be taken away before we get
a nosh or quick lick, whisked off into the mini-novas
of their flashing lights to a room that stinks of ether & mint.
The 1st responders of the world can spoil everything:
huge-footed & overwrought & flyophobic.

2

Since we taste w/our feet a stroll along *Samstrasse*
is a pleasant & diverting appetizer.
Dear Sam is fetally tucked into his sofa
(a bridge of sighs), incapable of playing
the noiseless, patient spider.

His stomach howls like a wolf!
He trembles (is he a-
cold? has winter already arrived,
a season that tolerates
neither him nor us?).

O there's the rub, bub————————————:
in the flyless time of year old folks drop like flies,
stagger in icy circles, groggy, weepy, multilayered,
huddled next to gas ranges, rolled up in rugs
——& the cold part is: when they d_e, they keep.

3

Mziz Lucasz, arms filled w/mysteries,
knocks, knocks, knocks. No need for reading matter, Mziz:
Sam's twixt murkiness & utter dark,
w/nose blueing & piss settling
& w/o the need for sleep (what's

more irrelevant now?)————& when
he steps over the boundary so will I,
vellicating his great white-meat prairie.
We'll conclude, end it all, the two of us.
He won't return.

I kind of will (*sumus ergo sum*).
We'll cross the bar together, wing in arm,
arm in wing. . . . . .going, going, gone.
Am not I a man like thee————————?
Or art not thou a fly like me————————?

Fly No. 7

1

He's d__d (at last) (alas): & what a joy it is now to
stroll, w/o fear of swatting, the boardwalk of his forearm,
the bunnyslope of his forehead,
the thatched roof of his temple.
Already our lovely females

are stuffing their *minaudières* w/eggs & making a flyline
for eye corners & underarms & various caves of the wind.
Sam is being eaten by our impolitic worms
————————& now he looks like 1 of them,
pale, pulpy, writhing w/the moon.

Already he rumbles under us: a mephitic flatus forms,
the skin tightens (prelude to meltdown),
cold & hard → hot & juicy & so the Fly Ball begins.
The sunlight microwaves him, bakes him from within.
He percolates, coddles, shirrs, steeps, caramelizes.

2
Speculative Note on Fly Heaven

He breathes, a mountain moving, but it's neither life
nor the soul
chugging out of the station, heading west
as it had (in theory) headed east
so many yrs ago. It's

only his chemistry escaping, his fumes slithering up,
corrugating the air * * * * * * *
* * * * * * * * * * * * * * * * You can
appreciate why there can't possibly be such things as fly souls.
If they existed they'd be gushing & popping

like champagne bubbles * * * * * * * * * & fly
heaven would be a world w/a census counted in powers,
a world so teeming nothing could penetrate it———an airless,
lightless, flightless eternity, a hereafter with so many eyes
& so little seeing.

3

Isn't it romantic: my inamorata/flyancée & I are w/moony
eyes sipping ⇨⇨⇨⇨ *Egri Bikave* ⇦⇦⇦⇦ while vealy Sam
is simmering, a *saltimbocca* jumping, & later green pillows of
strangolapreti + saffron pellets of *risotto milanese* +
a lumpy unflowing sea of *bolognese*:

but no dessert, TKU: too full: maybe a glass of port:
can't be logy: uninspired: too pooped to populate!
I'm stuffed to my propleuron————————————————————!
Sate, from OE *sadian*, akin to *sad*: & there is a sadness
about being sated, about reaching a state

of doneness, w/nowhere left to go————.
O my man Sam is
turning into a soft drink! A touch of fizz, built-in
digestivo. I can't down another morsel.
I can't eat. I can't eat. I can't eat. I eat.

4

We eat Sam, we = Sam: so what that weight must be,
what that paralysis & pain must be, that clenching
of the guts, that vine that catheters thru our veins
IS NOT from waiting for 911ers or from
the reports of sirens in the east——but IS the feeling

a fly was never intended to feel———: all alone. No
one was there for Sam. No one held his hand & whispered his name.
No one plumped his pillow & pushed back his
patch of hair. Now he's stew, soon to be soup,
a stain in the sofa—& what's the difference between

what he is & what he was? The human world goes on,
doesn't pause, doesn't look back, doesn't even know
it's missing 1 of its own. . . .at least there were no kneejerk words
of remorse, sniffling condolences, sobs of sorrow———:
altho even those would have been better than nothing.

5

We————the indifferent children of the earth,
D__h's pets, little black budgies too fat to fly
————————hear Mziz Stanko's *knock knock knock* & later
the earnest *thump thump thump* of 1st responders
& the *gulp gulp gulp* of their gagging (for

Sam is quite fragrant now, quite the calla lily).
They scoop him up like *gelato* & bring him to a dismal
room in a failing hospital & after leaving
leave it to Mziz S to disinfect w/squirts of yellow-green radiance
+ detonate another Ω Bomb, industrial-strength, as if

we were intruders, splinters in the world's
flesh————————————! Hey: we were here from the get-go,
here when no one else thought to drop by & chat
or bring over a meatloaf or a pound cake
or a pie, French apple, w/icing & fat black raisins.

Fly No. 8

Salut au Monde

Well, folks——————————————: it's been fun.
I speak for all flies past present & *pro re nata* & for our
good man, Sam, whose fly friends now number 5 or
6——tops——(all the others, sadly, have been Ω-ed
& lysoled into oblivion).

We hope you've enjoyed this glimpse into our world
& appreciated the opportunity to pay yr last respects
to dear Sam Jeden. The hour is late——————————.
We're starting to spin out of life & kick up a final fuss.
The children are already d__d in their beds

& so: * * * * * * * * * * * * * * *
* * * * * * * * * * * * * * * *
* * * * * * * * * * * * * * * *
* * * * * * * * * * * * * * * *

Good night, to you, dear reader (sweet sir or lovely lady).

Good night, fly palzz, including all the wee maggots.

Good night, bacteria & viruses, forks @ the ready.

Good night, locusts, screaming into the summer night.

Good night, dung beetles, sysiphean but not cheaters of D___h.

Good night, spiders: d_e, motherfuckers, in yr sleep.

Good night, silverfish, liquid knives under the sink.

Good night, mantises, murderous beasts & guides to the lost.

Good night, bees, hornets & wasps: where is thy sting?

Good night, fireflies w/yr warm/cold light.

Good night, fleas, loveless bloodsuckers.

Good night, Japanese beetles, fucking & eating, eating & fucking
(& maybe confusing the 2 now & then) from rising to setting sun.
Good night, *Eurychoromyia mallea*: rarest known fly (4 specimens
of which were collected in 1903 80 miles due north of La Pazz:
none has been seen since).

Good night, ants: earth is officially a formicarium.

Good night, cockroaches, fellow worshippers of D__h.

Good night, bats, unerring devourers of the "little flies."

Good night, worms & other crawling creatures: there must be

something interesting in yr lives that makes you keep living them.

Good night, gentle souls of the world who truly won't harm a fly.

Good night, good students, experts @ extrapolation.

Good night, dear lovers w/yr arms & legs in knots.

Good night, lonelyhearts w/whom the world's secrets are kept.

Good night, young people too shy to seek out each other.

Good night, insomniacs: & now to sleep.

Good night, unhappy souls separated by the vastness of space.

Good night, babushka ladies who know & have seen everything.

Good night, softball players: in 7 innings you find an ∞ of joy.

Good night, restaurant workers: flies ♥ you.

Good night, truck drivers: stay in yr own lane!

Good night, park attendants, the hosts of golden daffodils.

Good night, lifeguards: watch for the ones not shouting.

Good night, Good Humor vendors: toasted almond for everyone!

Good night, bartenders who watch as people turn into dreams.

Good night, Mr. Zzimmerman: consider a liqueur from melon gone bad.

Good night, barflies w/gin flowing thru the veins of their wings.

Good night, gardeners who make something of dull brown earth.

Good night, roses & lilacs perfuming the night w/their sighs.

Good night, tulips, lollipops for deer.

Good night, purple sweetpeas rising out of a sea of pachysandra
to touch the tops of trees.

Good night, catbird: in yr *rifacimenti* we hear our buzz.

Good night, robin: yr song is the morning & evening star.

Good night, dogs, stupid beasts, barking @ nothing.

Good night, Mziz Stanko's cat, brutal fly torturer &
murderer when there's nothing better to do.
Good night, Vincent Price: cinema god,
altho we can't watch movies (@ intervals of 1/200th/sec:
our vision does not persist & so, too quick

for the world, we more or less rule it————————).
Good night, lights, fridge, toilet, stove, pantry, sink, tub,
medicine cabinet: the landmarks of Mziz Stanko's realm.
Good night, sofa, still sighing.
Good night, Sam's junk, including TV w/foil (Al).

Good night, harbor w/the world slapping @ yr shore & boats.
Good night, harbormasters w/eyes that know the size of things.
Good night, mariners of the world, some in storm, some on watch.
Good night, fly fishermen who, we assume, don't fish for flies.
Good night, hunters: maybe *yr* herd will be thinned.

Good night, Perezz, sad-eyed & furious w/the world.

Good night, Mziz Lucasz: the mystery is solved.

Good night, grunting Wright, eternally internally clean.

Good night, mothers strolling along the boardwalk:

the incoming breezes are like hands under yr skirts.

Good night, Mziz Z_____: Sam thanks you & yr shorts.

Good night, fathers: yr children are yrs but not you.

Good night, 1st responders searching the world for pain & D__h.

Good night, hospital patients: make yr visitors feel @ ease.

Good night, doctors: show yr heartsickness.

Good night, nurses: never harden or look away.

Good night, artists: listen to everyone, heed only yrself.

Good night, poet: yes, you probably can do better than this.

Good night, writers & singers of songs: you won't go unheard for long.

Good night, sculptors: why not forge life-size flies?

Good night, editors & critics: assassins of orchids.

Good night, overzealous friends, authors of yr own loneliness.

Good night, young cynic: w/o heart & brain all you have is snot.

Good night, wealthy prick, you can't lose the soul you've never had.

Good night, couples, the love that lasts the longest is the sweetest.

Good night, librarian, the soft gentle voice that concludes

5,000+ yrs of shouting.

Good night, prisoners in prison: never stop being ashamed.

Good night, broken men & women: kindness rebuilds.

Good night, babies: we sing our songs in yr raw ears.

Good night, contralto, touching heaven in the organ loft.

Good night, carpenter w/eyelashes flecked beeleglike w/sawdust.

Good night, lunatic, asylum bound, no longer sleeping

in the extra room intended for guests who never arrive.

Good night, bride, throwing up on yr bridal gown.

Good night, policeman: yr job is difficult but you can do better.
Good night, printer w/teeth yellow & rootless from tobacco.
Good night, machinist, despising the white shirt over you.
Good night, salesgirl w/feet burning behind the counter.
Good night, attorney: for once, accept something on faith.

Good night, animal lovers: someday yr affection will include us.
Good night, children: ignore the stomp & bellow of monsters.
Good night, teachers: learn from every human's last day
& every fly's short journey & long memory.
Good night, priests, belching after pork loin roast & ale.

Good night, women who d_e for love when others live for it.
Good night, dreamers in whose dreams are found
color w/o light, sound w/o vibration, voices w/o mouths,
touch w/o feeling, worlds w/o matter.
Good night, old friends stuck in the black loam of the past,

soon yr heads, green & delicate, will greet the air.
Good night, old men & old women: forgive
the young their indiscretions & thoughtlessness;
after all, they can't always think of you.
Good night, uncles & aunts, cousins & friends, grandmothers

& grandfathers, sons & daughters: keep close, keep in touch.
Good night, moon & sun & stars & planets & asteroids.
Good night, everyone: make the signal, raise high the
open hand (&/or wing) of friendship———————!
Good night, good night, good night, good night————.

Fly No. 1

2 *Muscae sunt omnes divisae in partes tres*:

   All flies are divided into three parts.

   Sumus ergo sum

   We are therefore I am.

3 My man's rooms have been bugged, rebugged

   Herr Schwartzspinne

   A convoluted reference to Delmore Schwartz's poem,

   "The Spider." In German, spider is *das Spinne*.

Fly No. 2

3 L.S.M.F.T.

   An old cigarette slogan: Lucky Strike Means Fine Tobacco.

4 Le Poème de l'extase

   The title is taken from a symphonic work by the Russian

   composer Alexander Scriabin.

   time = slime,/ a runny camembert sliding by

   Dali used the phrase "the camembert of time and space" to

   describe the limp watches in *The Persistence of Memory* (1931).

9 TKU, Frau Schwartzspinne, for Killing Me

   A true acrostic/telestich spelling out HELPME, the fly/

   human's last words in *The Fly*.

Fly No. 3

1 *Sumus ergo sum*. I understood my man Sam to be a

> *the murmurous haunts*
> From Keats' "Ode to a Nightingale."

Fly No. 4

1 D___ly d___ly light, a medley of swattings (my

> *Res judicat*
> A thing already decided.

2 The bodycount is @ 15. *Res ipsa loquitor*: enough to make

> *Res ipsa loquitor*
> The thing speaks for itself.

> *kremska*
> A creamy type of Polish mustard.

3 The swatter is speckled

> *contrapasso*
> The idea that a punishment is an ironic comment on the sin
> or crime. For instance, in Canto 1 of the *Inferno*, Paolo and
> Francesca are blown about by whirlwinds, as out of control in
> Hell as they were on earth.

Fly No. 5

1 Muscae Volitantes

> The so-called floaters which people see because of fragments
> in the vitreous humor. The term means *flying flies*.

5 D___h Strikes Again

> *& when Orestes leaves,*
>
> *he takes w/him a city's sins, its d__d & its flies?*
>
> The finale, more or less, of Sartre's *Les Mouches.*

> *Fled is that wondrous music.*
>
> *Do I sleep or stay awake?*
>
> Based on the last line to Keats' "Ode to a Nightingale."

Fly No. 6

3 Mziz Lucasz, arms filled w/mysteries,

> *Am not I a man like thee————————?*
>
> *Or art not thou a fly like me————————?*
>
> From William Blake's "The Fly."

Fly No. 7

1 He's d__d (at last) (alas): & what a joy it is now to

> *our impolitic worms*
>
> *Hamlet* (IV, iii, 19-31)

3 Isn't it romantic: my inamorata/flyancée & I are w/moony

> *Egri Bikave*
>
> A dark Hungarian red wine. The name means "bull's blood."
>
> *saltimbocca*
>
> An Italian dish in which veal (or chicken) is sautéed with
>
> sage and prosciutto and served with a marsala sauce; it means
>
> "jumps in the mouth." *Strangolapreti* is a gnocchi made with
>
> spinach; the name means "priest strangler," because, as the

story goes, a priest thought the dish so delicious he nearly choked while eating it. *Risotto milanese* (risotto favored with saffron) and *ragù alla bolognese* (a thick rich meat sauce from Bologna) are other staples of Italian cuisine, which flies apparently love.

5 We———the indifferent children of the earth
intruders, splinters in the world's/flesh————————!
From Sartre's *Les Mouches*:
Tu n'es pas chez toi, intrus; tu es dans le monde
comme l'écharde dans la chair, comme le braconnier
dans la forét seigneuriale. . . .
(You are not at home, intruder; you're out in the world
like a splinter in the flesh, like a poacher
in the royal forest. . .)

Fly No. 8
Salut au Monde

assassins of orchids
Stolen from Frank O'Hara.

COLOPHON

Cover design and dead fly by John Edward Surowiecki

Typesetting by LMR
Titles set in Oswald
Text set in Hoefler
with help from the following:
Times
Symbol
Wingdings
Wingdings 3
Zapf Dingbats

Printed in an edition of 500
by McNaughton & Gunn, Inc. in Michigan

ABOUT THE AUTHOR

Flies is John Surowiecki's fourth book of poetry. The others are: *Barney and Gienka* (CW Books, 2010), *The Hat City after Men Stopped Wearing Hats* (Washington Prize, Word Works, 2006) and *Watching Cartoons before Attending a Funeral* (White Pine Prize, White Pine Press, 2003). He's also published six chapbooks, including two with Ugly Duckling Presse: *Mr. Z., Mrs. Z., J.Z., S.Z.* (2011) and *Further Adventures of My Nose* (out of print, but enjoying a second life as part of UDP's online chapbook archive).

In recent years, he has won the Poetry Foundation Pegasus Award for verse drama (his play, *My Nose and Me*, was based on the *Further Adventures of My Nose* chapbook), the Nimrod Pablo Neruda Prize, and he took the silver in the Sunken Garden National Competition.